Making a Model Sports Stadium

Sally Cowan
Photographs by Lindsay Edwards

Contents

Goal

To make a model of a sports stadium

Materials

You will need:

- a large white cardboard box, with sides 5–6 cm high

- yellow, purple, brown and green paints

- paintbrushes

- coloured pencils

- a sheet of white card, the same size as the bottom of the box

- glue

- five smaller sheets of card – black, white, yellow and blue

- scissors
- a ruler

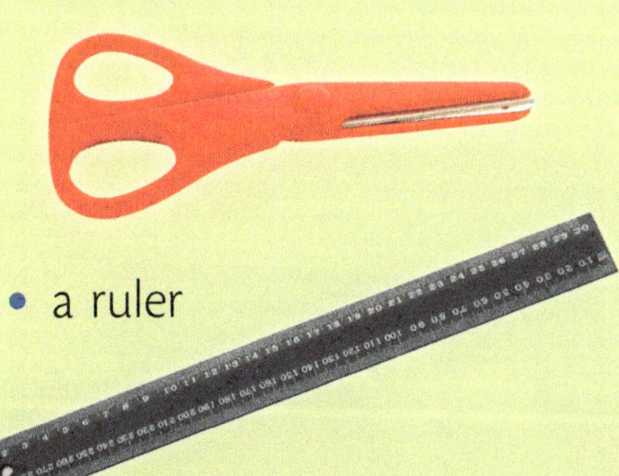

- tape

- four plastic straws

- a white marker pen.

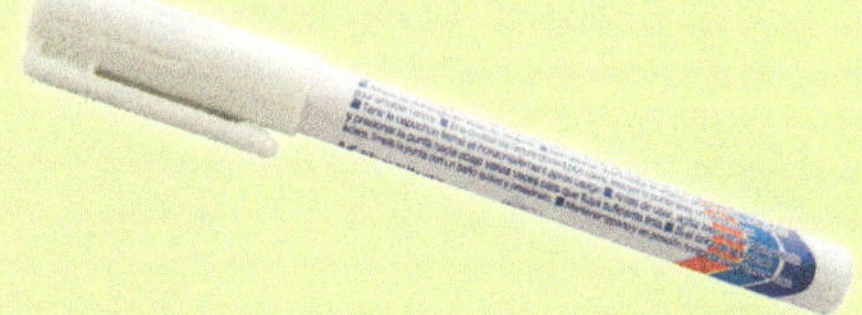

Steps

The Stadium

1. Paint the inside walls of the box yellow, and the outside walls purple. Let the paint dry.

2. Use a coloured pencil to draw a big doorway on one end of the box, to make the **entrance** to the stadium.

The Running Track

3. Use brown paint to mark an oval running track on the sheet of white card.

4. Paint the inside of the oval green. This will be for the field events.
5. Glue the sheet of card into the bottom of the box, with the painted side up.

The Winners' Podium

6. Use one of the small sheets of white card to make a **podium** for the winners.

   Cut a smaller square from the sheet of white card. Fold and glue the square of card into a long box. Each side will be the shape of a rectangle.

7. Cut a long strip from the other part of the card. Fold and glue this card into the shape of a **cube**.

8. Glue the cube onto the long box.

9. Glue the podium onto the oval, inside the track. The winner stands on the top of the podium.

The Grandstand

10. Use the yellow card to make the **grandstand**. Hold one end of the card, and turn the paper backwards and forwards, until it looks like a fan.

11. Open out the card and glue it to one end of the box. The folds will be the seats for the **spectators**.

The Stadium Lights

12. Use the ruler to draw a line
down the middle of the blue card.
Draw another line across the middle
to make four rectangles.
Cut along the lines.

13. Tape a straw to each rectangle.
These rectangles will be the stadium lights.

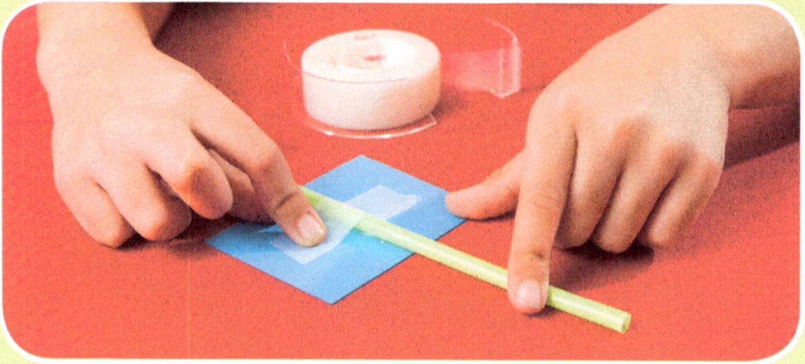

14. Glue a light to each corner of the stadium.

The Big Screen

15. Make a big screen with the black card.

16. Write the names of the winners on the screen with the white marker pen. You can choose the names!

17. Glue the screen onto the end of the box, facing the grandstand.

The Athletes

18. Draw and colour in five athletes on the last white card.

19. Cut around each athlete.
Leave a small tab of card by the feet of each athlete.

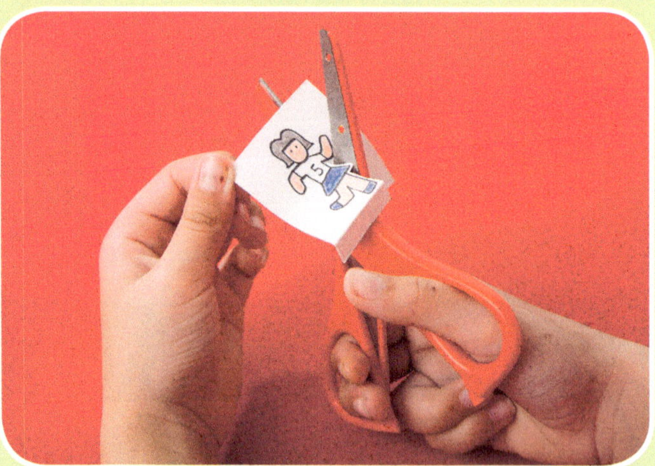

20. Bend the tabs back, and put glue on them.

21. Place the athletes on the running track in the stadium.

Now, your sports stadium is finished!

Glossary

cube *(noun)*	a shape like a box, with square sides
entrance *(noun)*	the way in to somewhere
grandstand *(noun)*	a big set of long seats like steps, for people watching a game
podium *(noun)*	a small stage that is higher than the ground
spectators *(noun)*	the people in the sports stadium watching the game